101 FACTS

ABOUT

Billie Eilish

Coloring, Quizzes, Journaling, and More!

Meet Billie Eilish

Billie Eilish Pirate Baird O'Connell, born on December 18, 2001, in Los Angeles, California, emerged into a world teeming with creativity and expression. Raised in a household brimming with artistic energy, Billie's childhood was infused with the melodies of her parents, Maggie Baird and Patrick O'Connell, both seasoned musicians and actors. From a young age, Billie showed an innate passion for music, often singing along to her parents' tunes and experimenting with melodies of her own. With her brother, Finneas, as her constant companion and creative collaborator, Billie embarked on a musical journey that would soon capture the hearts of millions around the globe.

The Road to Stardom:

Billie's journey from aspiring singer-songwriter to global sensation is a testament to her unwavering dedication and boundless talent. At just 13 years old, Billie and Finneas recorded "Ocean Eyes," a hauntingly beautiful track that would catapult them into the spotlight. Originally intended as a simple home recording, "Ocean Eyes" quickly went viral, captivating listeners with its ethereal sound and poignant lyrics. Overnight, Billie found herself thrust into the whirlwind world of fame, with fans clamoring for more of her mesmerizing music and magnetic presence.

Personal Influences:

Behind every great artist lies a tapestry of influences and inspirations, and Billie Eilish is no exception. Drawing from a diverse array of musical genres and styles, Billie's sound is a melting pot of eclectic influences, ranging from jazz and blues to hip-hop and electronica. Growing up, Billie was exposed to an eclectic mix of music, thanks to her parents' diverse tastes and the vibrant cultural landscape of Los Angeles. From the smooth crooners of the '50s to the boundary-pushing sounds of contemporary artists, Billie's musical palette is as varied as it is captivating.

Behind the Image:

In a world where image is often as important as artistry, Billie Eilish stands as a beacon of authenticity and self-expression. With her trademark oversized clothing, colorful hair, and bold accessories, Billie defies traditional notions of beauty and style, embracing her individuality with fearless confidence. Far from conforming to the pressures of the music industry, Billie uses her image as a canvas for self-expression, sending a powerful message of acceptance and empowerment to her legions of fans around the world.

Did You Know ?

- Billie Eilish was born Billie Eilish Pirate Baird O'Connell on December 18, 2001, in Los Angeles, California, amidst the twinkling lights of Hollywood.

- At just 11 years old, Billie wrote her first song, a poignant reflection of her youthful dreams and aspirations.

- The iconic neon-green hair that Billie sported was a spontaneous decision inspired by her desire to stand out in a sea of conformity.

Tunes and Tantrums: Billie's Journey into the Music World

In this section, we'll unravel the captivating tale of Billie Eilish's journey into the music world—a narrative marked by passion, perseverance, and the occasional tantrum. From her earliest musical experiments to the creation of her debut album, "When We All Fall Asleep, Where Do We Go?", we'll explore the highs and lows of Billie's ascent to superstardom.

Discovering the Muse:

Billie's love affair with music began at a tender age, as she found solace and inspiration in the melodies that filled her childhood home. With her parents' eclectic taste in music serving as her guide, Billie immersed herself in a world of sonic exploration, drawing inspiration from an array of genres and artists. From the soulful crooners of the past to the boundary-pushing sounds of the present, Billie's musical journey was shaped by a rich tapestry of influences that would later inform her own unique sound.

The Birth of "Ocean Eyes":

At the age of 13, Billie and her brother, Finneas, stumbled upon a musical gem that would change the course of their lives forever. Written and produced by Finneas, "Ocean Eyes" was a hauntingly beautiful ballad that showcased Billie's ethereal vocals and raw emotion. Originally intended as a song for Finneas' band, the track took on a life of its own when Billie recorded a mesmerizing vocal performance in their home studio. Released on SoundCloud in 2016, "Ocean Eyes" quickly went viral, captivating listeners around the world and laying the foundation for Billie's meteoric rise to fame.

Navigating the Industry:

As "Ocean Eyes" continued to gain traction, Billie found herself thrust into the fast-paced world of the music industry—a whirlwind of meetings, interviews, and promotional appearances. Despite her youth and relative inexperience, Billie approached each challenge with a fierce determination and unwavering confidence, refusing to compromise her artistic vision for the sake of commercial success. With her brother by her side as her creative collaborator and confidant, Billie navigated the highs and lows of the industry with grace and resilience, emerging stronger and more determined than ever to make her mark on the world.

The Making of "When We All Fall Asleep, Where Do We Go?":

In 2019, Billie released her highly anticipated debut album, "When We All Fall Asleep, Where Do We Go?", a genre-defying masterpiece that showcased her unparalleled talent and creative vision. From the eerie whispers of "bury a friend" to the anthemic chants of "bad guy," the album was a testament to Billie's fearlessness and willingness to push the boundaries of conventional pop music. Co-written and produced by Billie and Finneas, the album received widespread critical acclaim and cemented Billie's status as one of the most innovative and influential artists of her generation.

Zzzzzᶻᶻ ᶻ ᶻ z

Did You Know ?

- Billie's distinctive fashion sense, characterized by oversized clothing, is a deliberate statement against body shaming and societal norms.

- She's not just a singer-songwriter; Billie is also a talented dancer, mesmerizing audiences with her fluid movements on stage.

- Billie's love for animals is evident in her support for animal rights causes, often seen cuddling with rescue puppies backstage.

Activity: Stories in Sound

Billie Eilish's music resonates with a rare combination of raw emotion and youthful vigor, establishing her as an emblematic figure for today's youth. With each song serving as a window into her soul, Billie invites listeners to journey with her through the highs and lows of love, heartbreak, and self-exploration. In this section, we'll explore the captivating narratives behind some of Billie's most beloved tracks and offer readers an opportunity to channel their own creativity through songwriting exercises inspired by Billie's artistry.

"Bad Guy"

Story Behind the Song: Crafted from a place of playful rebellion, "Bad Guy" is a cheeky anthem that subverts traditional pop tropes with its dark humor and biting sarcasm. Billie's inspiration for the song stemmed from her desire to challenge societal norms and embrace her own quirks and imperfections.

Activity: Reflect on a time when you defied expectations or embraced your unique identity. Write a brief paragraph describing the experience and then craft a four-line chorus that captures the essence of your rebellion or individuality.

Date:

"When the Party's Over"

Story Behind the Song: Haunting and introspective, "When the Party's Over" delves into the themes of vulnerability and emotional exhaustion. Billie drew from her own experiences of feeling drained and overwhelmed, using the song as a cathartic outlet for her inner turmoil.

Activity: Reflect on a time when you felt emotionally drained or exhausted. Write a short paragraph describing the experience and then compose a four-line chorus that captures the raw emotion and vulnerability of that moment.

Date:

"Everything I Wanted"

Story Behind the Song: "Everything I Wanted" explores the pressures of fame and the desire for validation and acceptance. Inspired by Billie's own struggles with mental health and the pitfalls of celebrity culture, the song offers a candid glimpse into her psyche.

Activity: Consider a time when you felt the weight of expectations or the desire for validation from others. Write a paragraph reflecting on your experience and then craft a four-line chorus that conveys the longing for acceptance and understanding.

Date:

- Despite her meteoric rise to fame, Billie remains refreshingly down-to-earth, often spending her downtime playing with her pet tarantula, Charlotte.

- Billie's ethereal voice has been compared to that of an angel, capable of stirring emotions and touching souls with its haunting beauty.

- An avid painter, Billie finds solace in expressing her emotions through art, often channeling her inner turmoil onto the canvas.

Did You Know ?

- Billie's songwriting process often begins with late-night sessions in her bedroom, surrounded by fairy lights and her beloved ukulele.

- She's not just a music sensation; Billie is also a voracious reader, finding inspiration in the pages of classic literature and contemporary poetry.

Letter to Billie: Write a letter to Billie expressing your appreciation for her music and how it has impacted your life. Share personal stories or memories related to her songs.

 Date:

_____

_____

_____

_____

_____

_____

_____

_____

_____

_____

_____

_____

_____

_____

_____

_____

_____

- Billie's magnetic stage presence is fueled by her genuine connection with her fans, whom she affectionately refers to as her "lovely creatures."

- Despite her youthful age, Billie possesses a wisdom beyond her years, often imparting profound insights into the complexities of life and love.

- Billie's dedication to her craft is unwavering, spending countless hours perfecting her sound in the studio until every note resonates with authenticity.

- Behind the scenes, Billie is a self-proclaimed foodie, delighting in culinary adventures and experimenting with exotic flavors from around the world.

- Billie's musical influences range from the soulful melodies of Etta James to the raw energy of hip-hop, shaping her eclectic and genre-defying sound.

- She's not afraid to speak her mind; Billie uses her platform to advocate for social justice issues, championing causes close to her heart.

1. What is the title of Billie Eilish's debut single?

a) Bad Guy

b) Ocean Eyes

c) When the Party's Over

d) Lovely

2. Which music festival solidified Billie Eilish's status as a global phenomenon in 2019?

a) Glastonbury Festival

b) Coachella Valley Music and Arts Festival

c) Lollapalooza

d) Bonnaroo Music and Arts Festival

3. What is Billie Eilish's favorite holiday?

a) Christmas

b) Halloween

c) Thanksgiving

d) New Year's Eve

Answers:
1.b) Ocean Eyes
2.b) Coachella Valley Music and Arts Festival
3.b) Halloween

- Billie's bond with her brother, Finneas, goes beyond music; they share an unbreakable sibling connection forged through years of collaboration and creativity.
- A true free spirit, Billie finds inspiration in the beauty of nature, often escaping to the wilderness to recharge her creative energies.
- Despite her global fame, Billie remains fiercely independent, navigating fame on her own terms and staying true to her artistic vision.

- Billie's love for vintage fashion is a nod to the glamour of bygone eras, infusing her style with a timeless elegance and nostalgic charm.

- She's a fierce advocate for mental health awareness, using her own struggles as a platform to destigmatize discussions surrounding anxiety and depression.

"BE EXACTLY WHO YOU
WANT TO BE, DO WHAT
YOU WANT TO DO,
AND DON'T LET
ANYONE TELL YOU
OTHERWISE."

- **Billie Eilish**

- Billie is a night owl by nature, often finding inspiration and creativity striking in the quiet hours of the evening.

- Despite her fame, Billie is an introvert at heart, finding solace and introspection in quiet moments of reflection.

- Billie's dream collaboration is with legendary musician Paul McCartney, whom she admires for his timeless music and innovative songwriting.

- She's not just a musician; Billie is also a talented actress, bringing her unique blend of authenticity and emotion to the silver screen.

- Billie's love for vintage cars is a testament to her appreciation for craftsmanship and nostalgia, often seen cruising around town in her classic rides.

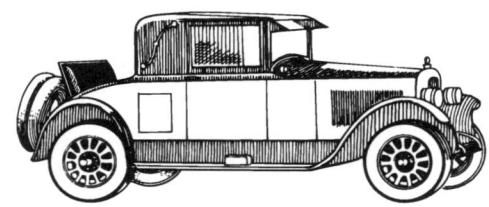

Inspired by Billie: Billie Eilish inspires people with her music. Write about something you've done that you feel proud of, inspired by Billie's messages of kindness and confidence.

 Date:

_____

_____

_____

_____

_____

_____

_____

_____

_____

_____

_____

_____

_____

_____

_____

_____

1. What was the title of the song that won Billie Eilish five Grammy Awards in 2020?
a) Bad Guy
b) Everything I Wanted
c) When the Party's Over
d) No Time to Die

2. which artist did Billie Eilish collaborate with for the song "Lovely"?
a) Khalid
b) Justin Bieber
c) Tyler, the Creator
d)) Lana Del Rey

3. What is the name of Billie Eilish's brother who often collaborates with her on music?
a) Finneas
b) Ethan
c) Noah
d) Liam

3. a) Finneas
2. a) Khalid
1. b) Everything I Wanted
Answers:

- Billie's love for horror films is reflected in her music videos, which often feature elements of the macabre and the supernatural.

- An advocate for self-expression, Billie encourages her fans to embrace their individuality and celebrate what makes them unique.

- Billie has a soft spot for rescue dogs, often using her platform to raise awareness for pet adoption and animal welfare.

- Billie's love for astrology is reflected in her music, which often explores themes of destiny, fate, and the cosmic mysteries of the universe.
- Billie's love for street art is evident in her music videos, which often feature vibrant murals and graffiti as a backdrop for her electrifying performances.

"EMBRACE YOUR QUIRKS
AND INDIVIDUALITY,
BECAUSE THAT'S WHAT
MAKES YOU UNIQUE AND
BEAUTIFUL."

- Billie Eilish

- In her free time, Billie enjoys exploring thrift stores and flea markets, hunting for unique vintage finds to add to her eclectic wardrobe.

- Billie's guilty pleasure TV show is "Friends," which she can binge-watch for hours on end, especially during lazy weekends.

- Billie's favorite subject in school was English, where she excelled in creative writing and poetry, showcasing her innate talent for storytelling.

Did You Know ?

- Despite her hectic schedule, Billie makes time for her passions, whether it's surfing at dawn or stargazing under the night sky.

- Billie's love for poetry is reflected in her lyrics, which are often imbued with vivid imagery and poignant symbolism.

- An advocate for environmental conservation, Billie uses her platform to raise awareness about the urgent need to protect our planet for future generations.

1. Which of the following is not a song from Billie Eilish's debut album "When We All Fall Asleep, Where Do We Go?"
a) Xanny
b) All the Good Girls Go to Hell
c) My Future
d) 8

2. What is the title of the documentary film about Billie Eilish released in 2021?
a) The World's a Little Blurry
b) When We All Fall Asleep, Where Do We Go?
c) The Billie Eilish Experience
d) Eilish: Behind the Music

3. What was Billie Eilish's age when she became the youngest artist to win all four major Grammy Awards in a single year?
a) 17
b) 18
c) 19
d) 20

- Billie's love for vintage cameras is evident in her photography, which captures the fleeting beauty of life with a timeless elegance.
- Billie Eilish's middle name, "Pirate," came from her brother's funny way of saying "pirate" when they were kids.

- Renowned for her signature style, Billie professes a deep affinity for the color blue, a hue that mirrors the depths of her creative soul.
- Billie perceives the world through a vivid spectrum of senses due to her synesthesia, which infuses her music with vibrant hues and textures.

"THE THOUGHT OF
BEING THE REASON
THAT SOMEONE SMILES
TODAY IS MIND-
BLOWING."

- Billie Eilish

- Billie's eclectic taste mirrors the multifaceted nature of her artistry, drawing inspiration from a diverse array of musical icons like Lana Del Rey and Tyler, the Creator.

- The inception of her meteoric rise, "Ocean Eyes," initially crafted for her brother's band, became the catalyst propelling Billie into the limelight.

- Billie's fascination with horror movies seeps into her artistic expression, adding an eerie allure to her music videos.

- Her first concert experience, attending Justin Bieber's electrifying performance with her mother, sparked the inspiration that later defined her own stage presence.

- Billie honors The Beatles through soulful renditions that bridge generational gaps with effortless grace.

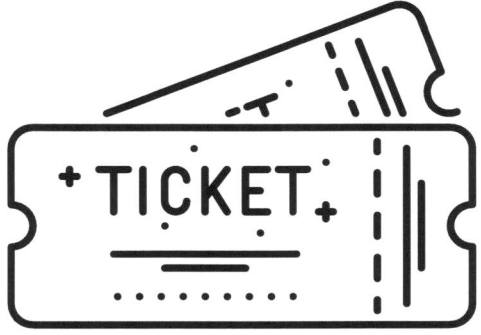

WORD SEARCH

```
S E W N E L Y T S E R F
O O M T P B S E U I E M
N S R M O E E Y R A X O
G I L I P N Y T A Z R A
W N A I E M E E R B C L
R G M X M Y N D T A I B
I E H A O I A G I D S U
T R R E C E E D S G U M
E G Q D Y G C E T U M P
R S N X S T O G W Y W I
```

Ocean Eyes   Grammy   Songwriter   Bad Guy
Singer   Pop   Style   Music   Artist   Album

Did You Know ?

- Collaborating with the legendary Takashi Murakami, Billie ventures into visual artistry, weaving surreal imagery into the mesmerizing music video for "You Should See Me in a Crown."

- From the lens of the supernatural emerges "Bury a Friend," a haunting masterpiece crafted from the shadows that haunt the corners of Billie's psyche.

- Billie was crowned with five Grammy Awards in 2020, including the coveted honors of Record of the Year and Album of the Year, Billie ascended to the zenith of musical excellence.

- Her haunting rendition of "No Time to Die" captivates audiences with its haunting beauty and emotional depth, Breaking barriers as the youngest artist to craft a James Bond theme song.

"YOU CAN'T ALWAYS WIN, BUT DON'T BE AFRAID OF MAKING DECISIONS."

- Billie Eilish

- Billie Eilish uses her platform to challenge societal norms and redefine the standards of beauty with unapologetic confidence, making her a fervent champion of body positivity.
- Billie's fashion choices, cloaked in oversized attire, empower her to reclaim her autonomy and self-expression, serving as a shield against the prying eyes of a judgmental world.
- At the forefront of advocating for racial equality, Billie lends her voice to the chorus of advocates demanding justice and social reform.

- Billie's music is woven with threads of vulnerability and resilience, embodying a tapestry of dark and introspective themes that deeply resonate with listeners.

- Confronting her fear of needles head-on, Billie's journey towards self-discovery is marked by courageous leaps of faith and unwavering determination.

1. Which music video of Billie Eilish features animation by the renowned artist Takashi Murakami?

a) Bad Guy

b) You Should See Me in a Crown

c) Bury a Friend

d) Ocean Eyes

2. Which song by Billie Eilish features the lyrics "Don't be cautious, don't be kind. You committed, I'm your crime"?

a) Bellyache

b) Copycat

c) My Future

d) Bad Guy

3. What is the name of the song by Billie Eilish that features a collaboration with rapper Vince Staples?

a) Bellyache

b) Watch

c) &Burn

d) Lovely

- Halloween is Billie's favorite holiday, celebrating the whimsical and the macabre, embracing the spirit of mischief and mayhem.

- Billie has a blooming flower tattoo etched upon her collarbone serving as a poignant symbol of growth, resilience, and the enduring beauty of the human spirit.

Song Reflections: Select a Billie Eilish song that resonates with you emotionally. Write a journal entry reflecting on why the song is meaningful to you and how it makes you feel.

 Date:

- Billie's affection for "The Babadook" reveals her penchant for the psychological depths of storytelling, making her a devotee of cinematic horror.
- Billie finds inspiration in the boundless imagination of Japanese storytelling and visual aesthetics, immersed in the fantastical realms of anime and manga.

"I DON'T WANT TO
TAKE FOR GRANTED
WHAT I HAVE,
BECAUSE IT'S VERY
RARE."

- Billie Eilish

WORD SEARCH

R	Y	N	L	Y	R	I	C	S	U	L	D
L	D	C	O	P	Y	C	A	T	U	J	A
N	D	X	F	I	N	N	E	A	S	D	K
D	R	U	S	D	L	W	A	T	C	H	F
C	F	Z	M	E	P	L	I	C	O	N	O
B	I	L	L	I	E	V	E	R	S	Y	F
E	H	C	A	Y	L	L	E	B	O	I	R
P	B	P	H	Y	E	N	Z	U	E	U	G
I	P	A	P	E	W	T	T	M	O	R	V
R	A	E	R	I	I	H	N	T	C	O	C

Finneas   Youth   Lyrics   Tour   Icon   Watch
Billievers   Bellyache   Rebellion   Copycat

- Billie's affection for the movie "The Babadook" reveals her penchant for the psychological depths of storytelling.

- Billie's eclectic shoe collection reflects her penchant for sartorial experimentation and fearless self-expression, serving as a collector of footwear treasures.

- "The Office" is her favorite television show, offering respite from the tumultuous waves of reality.

Billie's Bucket List:
Adventures and Dreams

In this section, we delve into the adventurous spirit of Billie Eilish. Let's take a look at some of the dreams she managed to accomplish and explore some of the dreams she hopes to achieve in her lifetime. From wild escapades to personal aspirations, Billie's bucket list is as diverse and dynamic as her music.

Skydiving Over a Tropical Paradise

Billie dreams of experiencing the ultimate adrenaline rush by skydiving over a breathtaking tropical paradise. Imagining the thrill of freefalling through the clear blue skies, she envisions the rush of wind against her skin as she takes in panoramic views of lush greenery and pristine beaches below.

Road Trip Across America

With a love for exploration and adventure. Billie yearns to embark on an epic road trip across America. From the bustling streets of New York City to the serene landscapes of the Pacific Northwest. she dreams of traversing the vast expanse of the country. immersing herself in its diverse cultures and landscapes along the way.

Perform at Glastonbury Festival

Billie achieved one of her lifelong dreams by gracing the iconic stage of the Coachella Valley Music and Arts Festival, one of the largest and most renowned music festivals in the world. Amidst the electrifying atmosphere and the sea of adoring fans, she delivered a mesmerizing performance that transcended boundaries and captivated hearts.

Travel to Space

Ever the dreamer, Billie entertains the idea of venturing beyond the confines of Earth and traveling to space. Envisioning the vastness of the cosmos and the boundless possibilities of interstellar exploration, she dreams of experiencing weightlessness and gazing upon distant galaxies, letting her imagination soar to new heights.

- Billie's fear of sharks serves as a testament to the awe-inspiring majesty and primal allure of the sea, engulfed in the depths of oceanic mysteries.
- Billie's fashion sense, cloaked in the streetwise allure of Supreme and Off-White, embodies the ethos of urban cool, blending high fashion with underground edge.

Discover Your Soundtrack: List Your Top Ten Billie Eilish Songs

On this page, jot down your top ten Billie Eilish tunes. Dive into the melodies that resonate with your soul and capture your experiences. Let Billie's music be the backdrop to your journaling journey.

- "The Sims" is Billie's favorite video game, offering boundless opportunities for creative expression and imaginative exploration, immersed in the whimsical world of digital escapism.

- She has a pet pit-bull named Shark, Billie finds solace and companionship in the loyal embrace of her four-legged friend.

- Billie's passion for home decor reflects her penchant for curating spaces that echo the rhythms of her eclectic personality, making her a maestro of interior design.

- Billie's dance moves exude a captivating blend of grace and dynamism, transforming her performances into mesmerizing spectacles of movement and rhythm, transcending the confines of the stage.

Visual Vibes: Billie's Most Iconic Music Videos

In this section, we take a deep dive into the mesmerizing world of Billie Eilish's music videos. From haunting visuals to bold artistic statements, each video is a visual masterpiece that enhances the storytelling of her music and showcases her unique creative vision.

"bad guy"

Directed by Dave Meyers, the music video for "bad guy" is a surreal journey through Billie's twisted imagination. With its quirky choreography, vibrant color palette, and offbeat humor, the video perfectly captures the playful yet enigmatic essence of the song.

"lovely" (with Khalid)

Directed by Taylor Cohen, the music video for "lovely" is a cinematic masterpiece that transports viewers into a world of haunting beauty and emotional intensity. From its opening frames, the video sets a somber tone, with Billie and Khalid situated in dimly lit rooms, surrounded by shadows that mirror the weight of their emotions.

"Happier Than Ever"

Directed by Billie Eilish herself, the music video for "Happier Than Ever" is a bold and cathartic experience. It takes viewers on a twisted journey through a suburban nightmare, with Billie transforming from a vulnerable young woman to a powerful avenging angel. The video's use of fire, unsettling imagery, and dark humor reflects the song's themes of heartbreak, betrayal, and ultimately, self-empowerment.

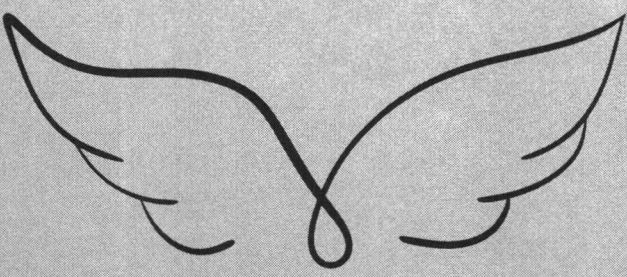

"Therefore I Am"

Directed by BRTHR, the music video for "Therefore I Am" is a playful and satirical commentary on social media culture. Filled with fast-paced cuts, vibrant colors, and quirky humor, the video finds Billie roaming a flooded mall, seemingly mocking the materialistic and superficial aspects of online life. The video's ending with Billie submerged underwater adds a layer of mystery and intrigue.

WORD SEARCH

```
C E L E B R I T Y C S M L
E K L T R A U J P N R U O
P E R F O R M A N C E S V
D I L A H K R F T G I I E
S S E C C U S L P N U C L
I N T E R V I E W I E I Y
F A S H I O N C A R Y A M
H N E M O Y C O E U V N O
Y I S U B R P A F O S U I
H A F E Q L R F M T F E E
P A R T Y F A V O R Z P X
```

Interview   Performance   Party Favor

Success   Celebrity   Musician   Fashion

Khalid   Touring   Lovely

"I DON'T WANT TO BE
IN THE SPOTLIGHT
BECAUSE I'M FAMOUS. I
WANT TO BE IN THE
SPOTLIGHT BECAUSE
I'M GOOD AT WHAT I
DO."

- Billie Eilish

Create Your Own Lyrics: Use Billie Eilish's songs as inspiration to write your own lyrics. Channel your thoughts and emotions into creating a song of your own.

 Date:

_____

_____

_____

_____

_____

_____

_____

_____

_____

_____

_____

_____

_____

_____

_____

_____

_____

_____

- Billie's favorite childhood toy was a stuffed animal named Mr. Snuggles, who accompanied her on many imaginative adventures.
- Despite her fame, Billie remains grounded by her close-knit family, often spending quality time with them over homemade dinners and board game nights.

Did You Know ?

- Billie's favorite childhood memory is spending summers at her grandparents' house, playing in the backyard and picking fresh fruit from their garden.

- Billie's favorite song to perform live is "Bellyache," which she describes as having an electrifying energy that always gets the crowd going.

- Billie's favorite way to unwind after a long day is with a hot bubble bath and her favorite soothing playlist, allowing her to relax and recharge.

"I WANT TO BE THE VOICE OF PEOPLE
WHO ARE SCARED TO SPEAK
UP.WHETHER IT'S MENTAL HEALTH,
BODY IMAGE, OR SOCIAL JUSTICE, I
WANT TO BE A VOICE FOR THE
VOICELESS AND A SOURCE OF
COMFORT AND INSPIRATION FOR THOSE
WHO NEED IT MOST."

- Billie Eilish

Did You Know ?

- Billie has a hidden talent for baking, often surprising her friends and family with delicious homemade cookies and cakes.

- An avid reader, Billie's favorite book is "The Catcher in the Rye" by J.D. Salinger, which she credits with shaping her perspective on life and art.

- Billie's go-to comfort food is a classic grilled cheese sandwich, perfectly crispy on the outside and gooey on the inside.

Billie Eilish's Secret Diary: Imagine you found Billie's secret diary. What do you think she would write about? Write a pretend entry from her diary about one of her exciting adventures.

Date:

_____

_____

_____

_____

_____

_____

_____

_____

_____

_____

_____

_____

_____

_____

_____

_____

"I DON'T LIKE TO BE LABELED AS 'THE TEENAGE POP STAR.' I WANT TO BE 'BILLIE EILISH THE ARTIST.' I DON'T WANT PEOPLE TO FOCUS ON MY AGE OR MY GENDER OR ANY OTHER SUPERFICIAL LABELS. I WANT THEM TO FOCUS ON MY MUSIC AND MY ARTISTRY. THAT'S WHAT'S MOST IMPORTANT TO ME."

- Billie Eilish

The Future's Bright: What's Next for Billie?

As Billie Eilish continues to captivate audiences around the globe with her unparalleled talent and innovative artistry, fans eagerly anticipate what the future holds for this groundbreaking artist. In this section, we explore the exciting prospects and upcoming projects on the horizon for Billie Eilish.

New Music

With each release, Billie Eilish pushes the boundaries of music, challenging genre conventions and defying expectations. Fans can look forward to eagerly anticipated new singles, albums, and collaborations that promise to showcase her evolving sound and unparalleled creativity. Whether she's crafting haunting ballads or infectious pop anthems, one thing is certain: Billie's music will continue to resonate with listeners on a profound level.

World Tours and Live Performances

As a dynamic performer with an electrifying stage presence, Billie Eilish is renowned for her unforgettable live shows. Fans can expect to see her take to the stage once again, performing her chart-topping hits alongside new and unreleased tracks. From intimate club gigs to massive stadium spectacles, Billie's live performances are not to be missed, offering fans a chance to experience her music in a whole new light.

Film and Television

With her boundless talent and magnetic screen presence, Billie Eilish is poised to make waves in the world of film and television. Whether she's lending her voice to animated characters, starring in her own documentary projects, or making cameo appearances in blockbuster films, Billie's foray into the world of visual storytelling promises to be as captivating as her music.

Philanthropic Endeavors

As a passionate advocate for social justice and environmental causes, Billie Eilish uses her platform to effect positive change in the world. Fans can expect to see her continue her philanthropic efforts, raising awareness and funds for causes close to her heart. From environmental conservation to mental health advocacy, Billie's commitment to making a difference inspires fans to join her in creating a better world for future generations.

"I'M NEVER GOING TO STOP WRITING MUSIC. EVEN IF NO ONE EVER HEARS IT, I'M GOING TO KEEP WRITING. IT'S MY WAY OF EXPRESSING MYSELF AND MAKING SENSE OF THE WORLD."

- Billie Eilish

Gratitude Journal: Write down three things you're grateful for today. It could be something related to Billie Eilish, like her music making you happy, or something else entirely.

 Date:

_____

_____

_____

_____

_____

_____

_____

_____

_____

_____

_____

_____

_____

_____

_____

_____

Made in the USA
Columbia, SC
04 September 2024

41731158R00054